For Esme, with love

IMAGE CREDITS

- Índios isolados no Acre (2009) — Photo by Gleilson Miranda / Governo do Acre, shot 9 Jul 2009. Source: Wikimedia Commons (File: Índios isolados no Acre 12.jpg). License: CC BY 2.0. Wikimedia Commons
- Korowai Treehouse (Papua) — Photo © George Steinmetz, featured in "The Lost Treehouses of Papua New Guinea" on My Modern Met, published 28 Nov 2012. Rights: All rights reserved (editorial feature). Wikimedia Commons
- "The Lost Treehouse Tribes of the Rainforest" — Article by Messy Nessy (MessyNessyChic), published 27 Sep 2021; images within credited to respective owners. Rights: article © publisher; image rights as credited in-article. Messy Nessy Chic
- Papuan Mummy — Photo by Ernamas (uploader/photographer), 28 Jan 2011. Source: Wikimedia Commons (File: Papuan Mummy.jpg). License: CC BY-SA 4.0. id.m.wikipedia.org
- Curaray River (Ecuador) — Photo by "Captain Phoebus" (enwiki), uploaded 26 Jul 2007. Source: Wikimedia Commons (File: Rio Curaray, 2007.jpg). License: dual-licensed GFDL 1.2+ and CC BY-SA 3.0 / CC BY 2.5 (per page). Wikimedia Commons+1
- "Faith and tragedy in the jungle: 69 years after the sacrifice of five missionaries in Ecuador" — News feature, Christian Daily International, 8 Jan 2025. Rights: © publisher; images within © their respective owners. www.christiandaily.com
- Manu National Park riverbank (Peru) — Photo by As578; taken before 29 Jul 2007 (transferred from enwiki). Source: Wikimedia Commons (File: Manu_riverbank.jpg). License: as specified on file page (Commons free license). Wikipedia+1
- "The Putumayo — the devil's paradise..." (1913) — Scanned illustration from W.E. Hardenburg's 1913 book; image provided by Internet Archive Book Images. Source: Wikimedia Commons (Flickr Commons scan). Rights: No known copyright restrictions / public domain. Wikimedia Commons
- "Enslaved natives with a load of rubber..." (Putumayo, 1910) — Photo by Roger Casement, 30 Oct 1910. Source: Wikimedia Commons. Rights: Public domain (author died 1916; pre-1930 publication). Wikimedia Commons
- Latex collection (rubber tapping) — Photo by Vis M, 17 Dec 2021. Source: Wikimedia Commons (File: Latex collection 05.jpg). License: CC BY-SA 4.0. Wikimedia Commons
- "The Peruvian State will face the Inter-American Court of Human Rights..." — Article by EarthRights International (ERI). Rights: © ERI; any photos in the story credited in-article. EarthRights International.
- USAID Measuring Impact / IGCP (Uganda) — USAID photo from a 2017 "Conservation Enterprise Retrospective" (Nkuringo, Uganda). Source: Wikimedia Commons (File: … (39582154334).jpg) in category "Nkuringo, Uganda." License: Commons free license shown on file page (typically CC BY 2.0 on USAID sets). Wikimedia Commons
- Dayak warrior with skulls (Borneo) — Photo from the Tropenmuseum / National Museum of World Cultures; authorship attributed to Charles Hose (early 1900s, c. 1900–1912). Source: Wikimedia Commons (Tropenmuseum collection). License: CC BY-SA 3.0 (museum release). Wikimedia Commons
- "Young Ibans, or Sea Dayaks" — Photo by Charles Hose; taken 1912, published 1922 in *Peoples of All Nations*. Source: Wikimedia Commons. Rights: Public domain (US). Wikimedia Commons
- Dajaks before a longhouse — Tropenmuseum / National Museum of World Cultures (Dutch collection). Source: Wikimedia Commons (file title begins "COLLECTIE TROPENMUSEUM Dajaks voor een langhuis..."). License: CC BY-SA 3.0 (museum release). Wikimedia Commons
- *Le Tour du monde* (vol. 14), p.129 (cropped) — 19th-century engraving/illustration from *Le Tour du Monde*. Source: Wikimedia Commons (File: Le Tour du monde – 14 (page 129 crop).jpg). Rights: Public domain (published before 1929). Wikipedia
- Aldeia Caxinauá no Acre (Huni Kuin) — Portuguese Wikipedia page (image within credited on Commons). Source: ptwiki "Aldeia Caxinauá no Acre – Huni Kuin". License: per individual image credit on page.
- Ishi — 1912 — Portrait of Ishi (Yahi), 1912. Source: Wikimedia Commons (File: Ishi – 1912.jpg). Rights: Public domain (US). Wikimedia Commons
- Ishi (First Captive Day), 29 Aug 1911 — Unknown photographer; first day in custody. Source: Wikimedia (file page on enwiki/Commons). Rights: Public domain (US).

All efforts have been made to attribute all the images used in this book.

The World's Wildest Tribes (2025) is part of the series 'Dr. Joffrey's Edgy Books' © James Frankcom

CONTENTS

The Lonely Island	8
Treetop Cannibals	12
Jungle Assassins	16
Freedom fighters	20
The Little People	24
Head Hunters	26
First Contact Stories	30
Glossary	38

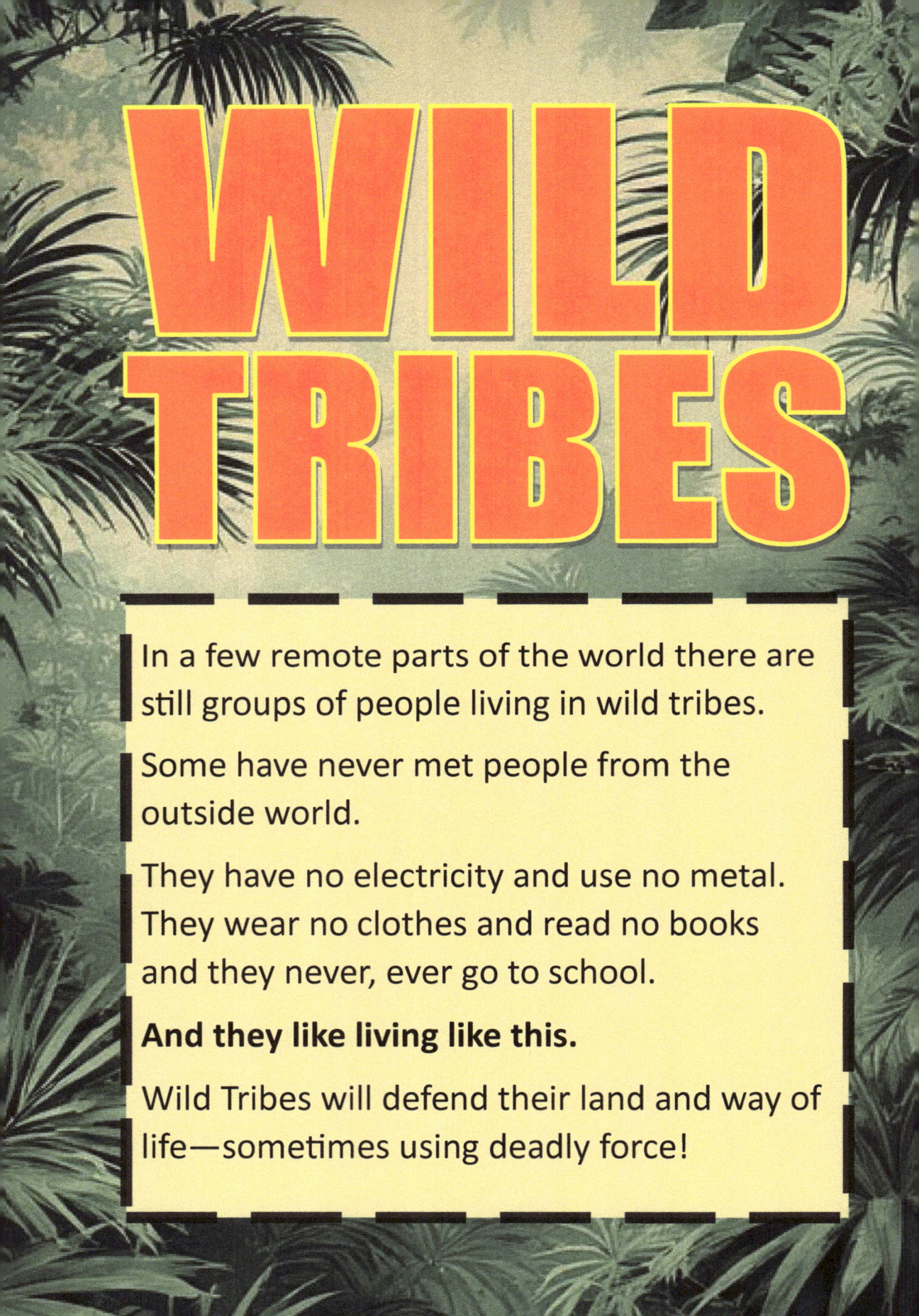

Wild Tribes are part of nature.

They have to find everything they need in the forest. They hunt for all the meat they eat, gather fruits and herbs and make their homes from leaves and branches.

This wild tribe were photographed using a long-distance camera based a mile away.

THE SENTINELESE

Population: 500

This tribe live on North Sentinel Island.

This small island is found in the Bay of Bengal, which is part of the Indian Ocean.

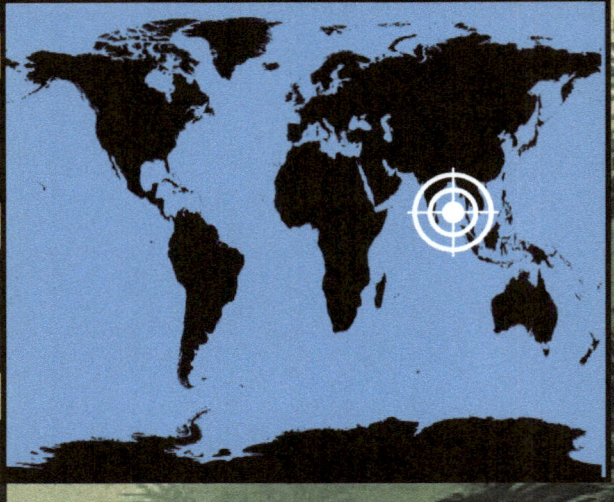

North Sentinel

Their island home is covered by a jungle full of birds and animals.

It is surrounded by a coral reef teeming with fish to hunt and eat.

The Sentinelese are **extremely hostile**. No outsider has ever been to their island and lived long enough to tell the tale!

In 1981 a cargo ship called MV Primrose was caught in a storm and became stuck on the reef around North Sentinel Island.

The trapped crew saw the Sentinelese tribe gathering on the beach armed with axes and clubs.

In the end the terrified crew were rescued by a helicopter!

In 2006 there was a more deadly encounter when two Indian fishermen fell asleep and their boat drifted too close to the island.

They woke to find themselves being attacked with axes and clubs. Sadly they were killed, and their bodies have never been found.

The Sentinelese are experts at fishing and hunt using canoes.

The Sentinelese are thought to be related to other people living on some nearby islands.

These people are the Andamanese and they made contact with explorers a long time ago. Sadly most of them have died out.

We know the Andamanese used to worship their ancestors, so it is possible the Sentinelese do this too.

Explorers reported that the Andamanese would carry the decorated skulls of their dead relatives around with them.

This man (right) is carrying the skull of his dad.

THE KOROWAI

Population: 4000

This tribe live in New Guinea— a mysterious island covered in swamp and jungle that is close to Australia.

New Guinea Highlands

New Guinea is home to hundreds of tribes that all speak different languages.

Some parts of the island are still unexplored.

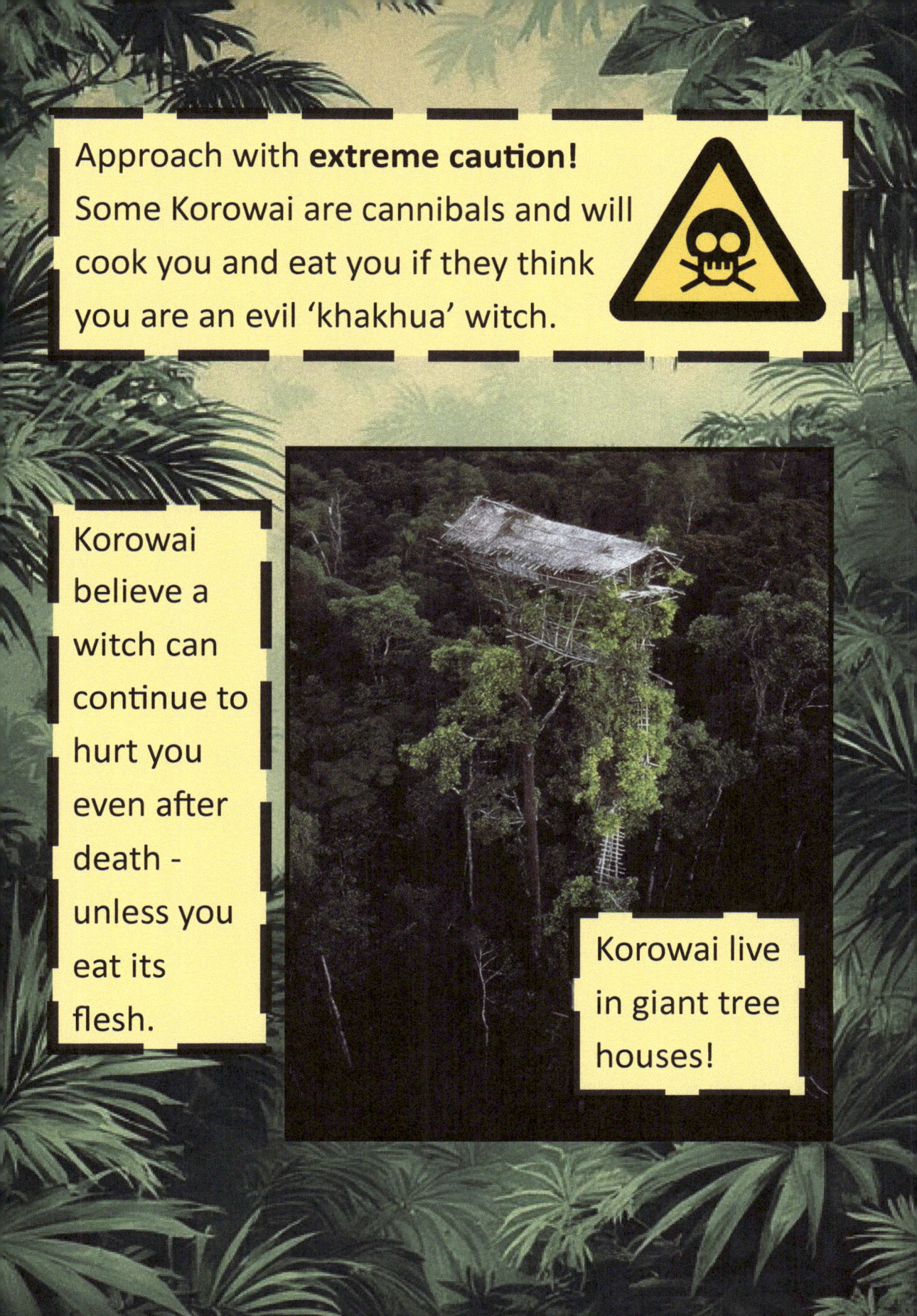

Approach with **extreme caution!** Some Korowai are cannibals and will cook you and eat you if they think you are an evil 'khakhua' witch.

Korowai believe a witch can continue to hurt you even after death - unless you eat its flesh.

Korowai live in giant tree houses!

The Korowai are just one tribe in New Guinea.

There are thousands of tribes speaking hundreds of different languages.

New Guinea is the second largest island in the world.

Some parts of it are still unexplored, and some tribes are still uncontacted.

Instead of burying their leaders, some New Guinea tribes use smoke to mummify them.

They build a special fire and the dead body is placed above the smoke, not in the flames.

The smoke slowly dries the body and keeps away bugs to stop it from rotting.

In the end, the body becomes dry and hard, like wood.

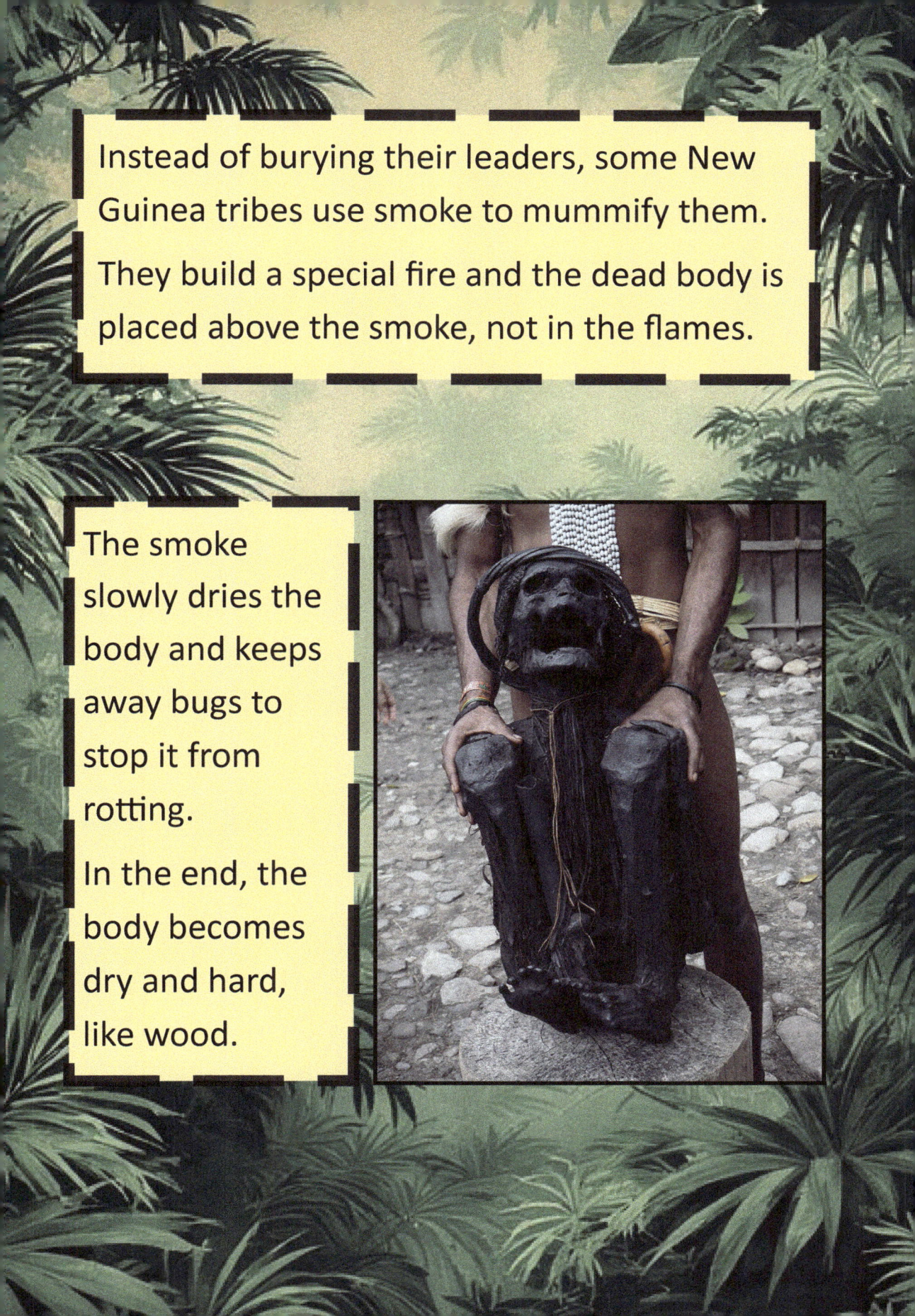

THE TAGAERI

Population: 30

The Tagaeri live deep in the hot, tropical forests of Ecuador in South America.

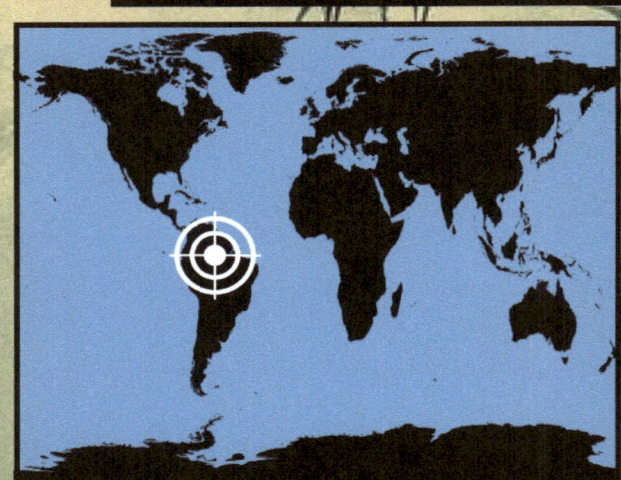

They live in small thatched houses built in remote forest clearings.

They wear almost nothing at all.

The Tagaeri used to be members of the larger Waorani tribe but they split off from them and formed their own tribe because they did not want to have any contact with outsiders.

Waorani hunters

DANGER! The Tagaeri are known to attack and kill any outsiders who approach their homelands.

The Tagaeri avoid outsiders because they are often attacked by **poachers** and loggers.

Also, outsiders accidentally carry deadly diseases which can spread to tribal people like Tagaeri and kill them.

Nate Saint in 1956

In 1956 a group of five **missionaries** led by Nate Saint travelled to Tagaeri land to try to make the tribe become Christians.

The missionaries hoped the Tagaeri would want to learn about Jesus—but they did not. All five men were speared to death soon after they had landed in their airplane.

In 1984, another missionary died trying to spread his religion to the Tagaeri.

The body of Alejandro Labaka was found pierced with many spears.

THE MASHCO-PIRO

Population: 750

The Mashco-Piro are a wild tribe of the Amazon living in eastern Peru and parts of Brazil.

This tribe has been coming out of the rainforest more frequently in recent years.

People are wondering if they are ok.

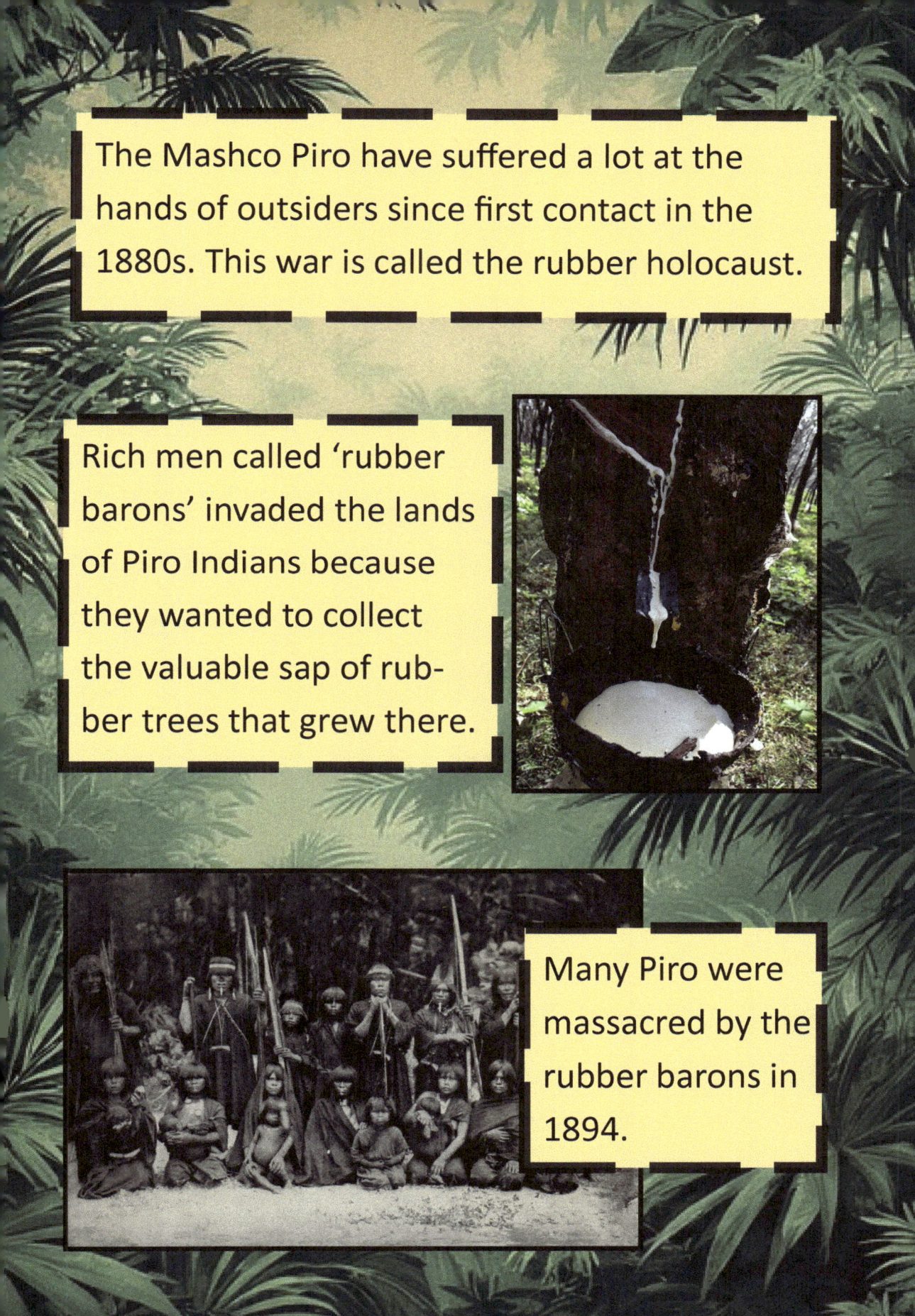

The Mashco Piro have suffered a lot at the hands of outsiders since first contact in the 1880s. This war is called the rubber holocaust.

Rich men called 'rubber barons' invaded the lands of Piro Indians because they wanted to collect the valuable sap of rubber trees that grew there.

Many Piro were massacred by the rubber barons in 1894.

The few survivors were forced to work on the rubber barons' **plantations** as slaves.

Slaves carrying rubber

Some Piro escaped from these horrors and hid in the remotest areas of the rainforest. These "free" Piro are now the called *Mashco* Piro. Although slavery ended in 1913, the Mashco Piro have stayed away.

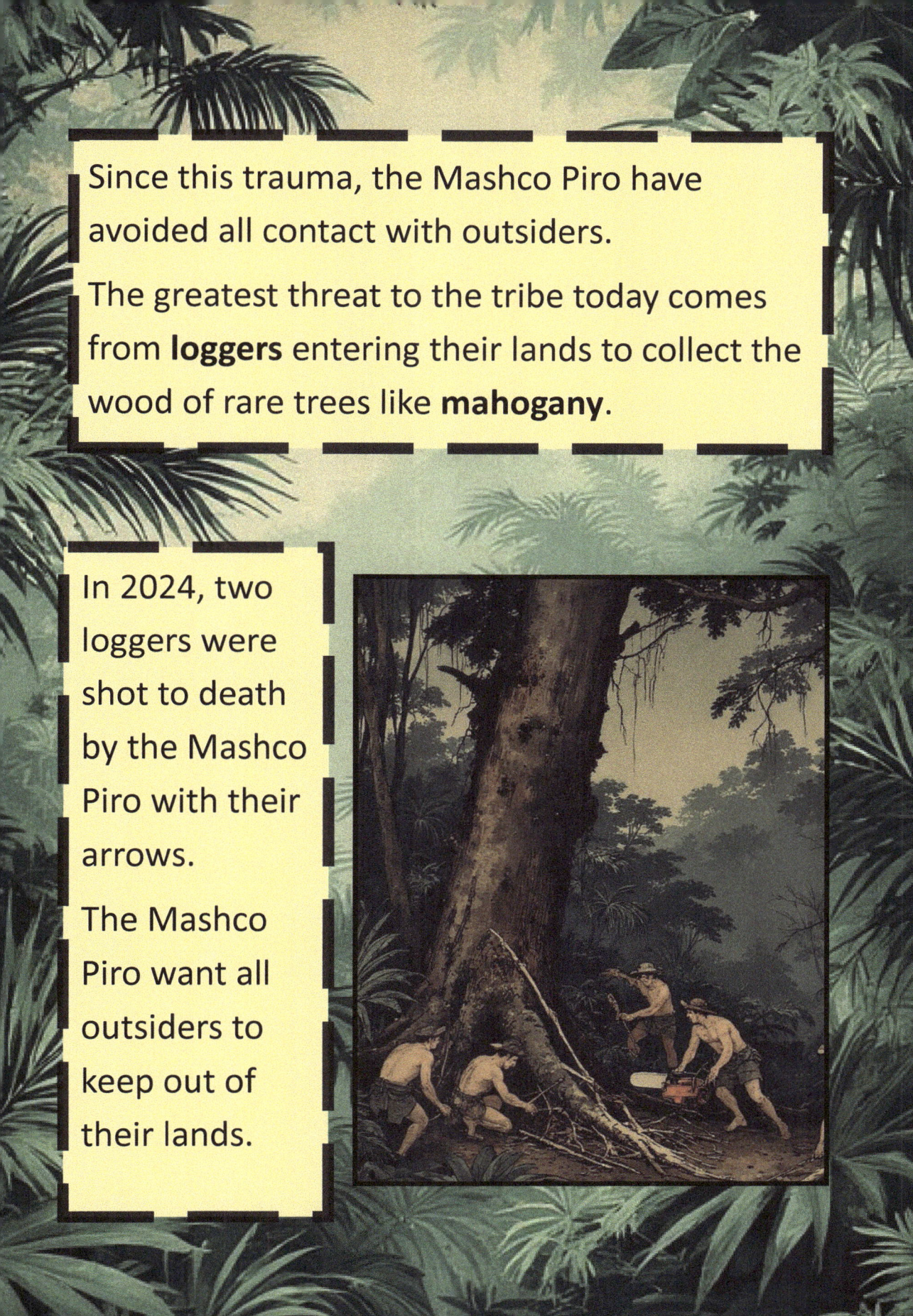

Since this trauma, the Mashco Piro have avoided all contact with outsiders.

The greatest threat to the tribe today comes from **loggers** entering their lands to collect the wood of rare trees like **mahogany**.

In 2024, two loggers were shot to death by the Mashco Piro with their arrows.

The Mashco Piro want all outsiders to keep out of their lands.

THE BAKA

Population: 10,000

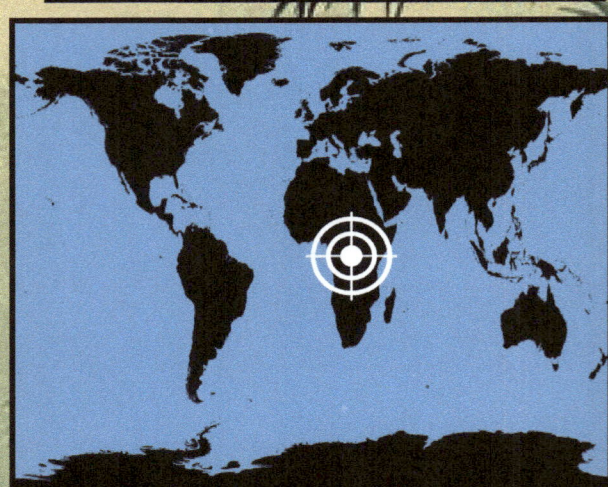

The Baka are a tribe of 'pygmies' that live in the rainforests of Congo and Gabon.

Tribes of pygmies live in many parts of central Africa.

They are called 'pygmies' because they are usually shorter than most other people when fully grown.

The Baka are peaceful people who live in the forest. They see the forest as their mother and father because it provides food, shelter and protection. The Baka believe the forest is inhabited by clever spirits called Jengi that can help them.

The Baka are known for their amazing singing voices that sound like the birds and animals of the forest. The Baka like to live in remote places.

THE BALEH IBAN

Population: 20,000

The Baleh Iban are a remote tribe that used to be terrifying warrior head-hunters.

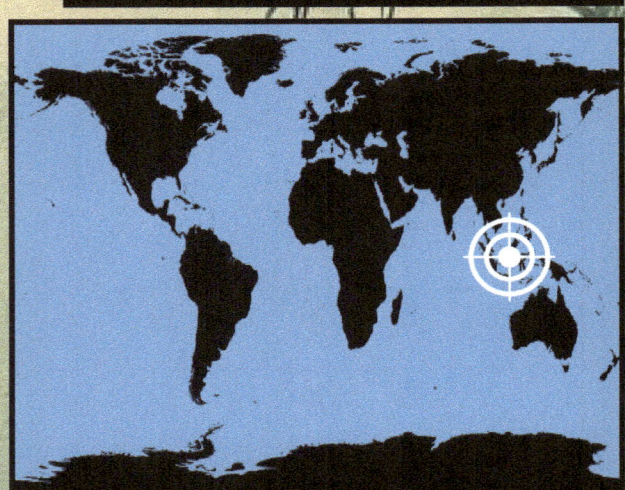

The Iban live in the jungles of Sarawak in South East Asia.

The Baleh Iban are the most traditional Iban community that still exist today. They still keep many of their ancient traditions.

The Baleh Iban were the last group of Iban to end their head-hunting raids. In 1869, the British Army invaded their lands and forced them to end their head-hunting raids.

Before a raid, Iban warriors would first perform wild dances. Then the warriors would go out on the raid carrying special swords called 'mandau'. They would use the mandau to cut off enemy heads.

The head would be smoked over a special fire to preserve it and then decorated with beads

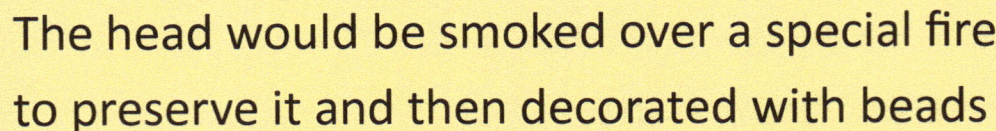

When it was ready the head would be paraded around the village and officially welcomed into the community with dancing and singing. It was then hung up inside the community longhouse for use in rituals.

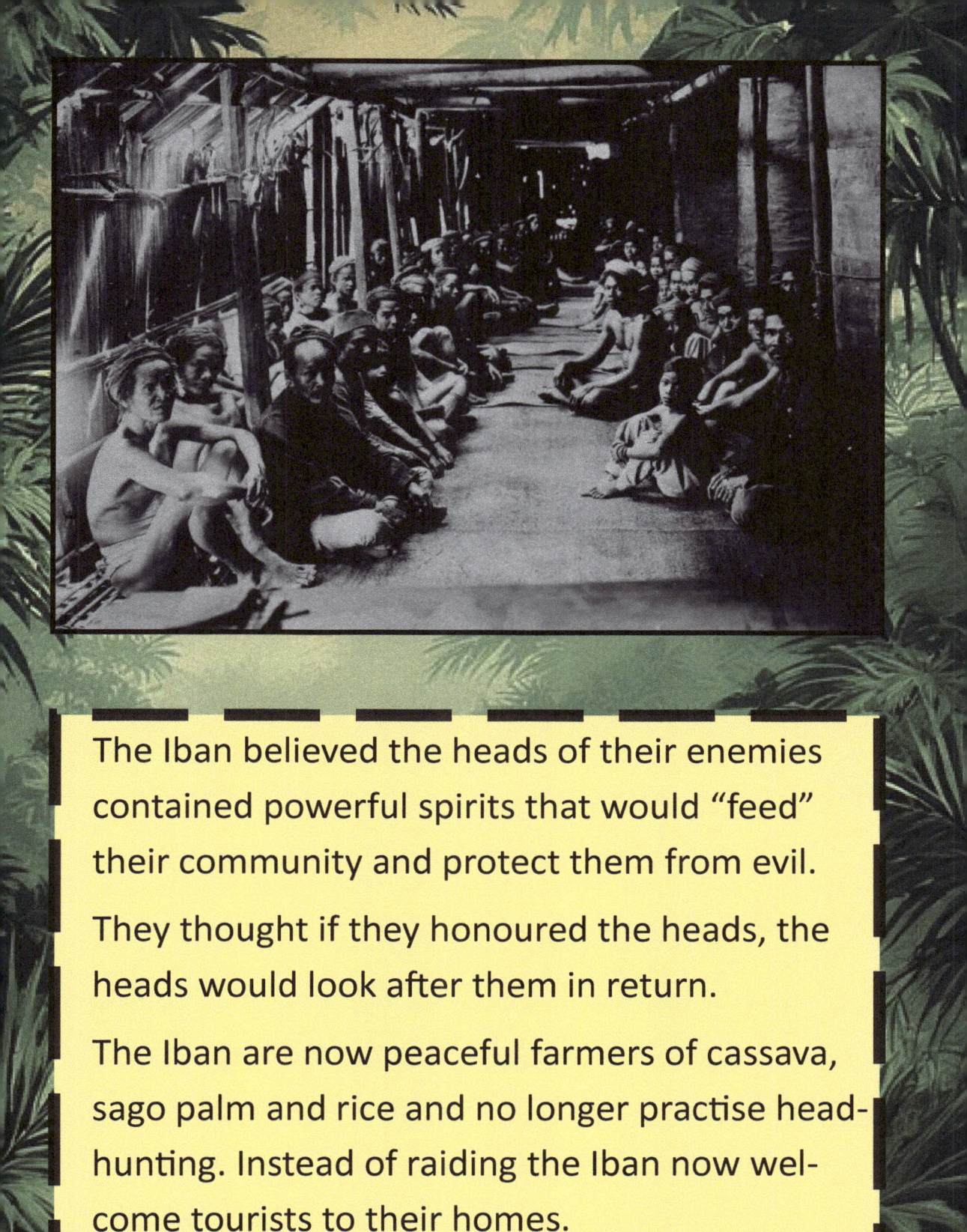

The Iban believed the heads of their enemies contained powerful spirits that would "feed" their community and protect them from evil.

They thought if they honoured the heads, the heads would look after them in return.

The Iban are now peaceful farmers of cassava, sago palm and rice and no longer practise head-hunting. Instead of raiding the Iban now welcome tourists to their homes.

FIRST CONTACT STORIES

Some tribes have never met people from the outside world. They are uncontacted.

Occasionally these uncontacted tribes meet people from the outside world. The first time this happens it is called making **first contact**. First Contact is a very dangerous and unpredictable event.

Over the next few pages you can read real stories about tribes making first contact.

THE MAN WITH NO NAME

First Contact: 1911

Ishi was the last living member of the Yahi tribe of Native Americans.

In 1911 he made first contact with the outside world.

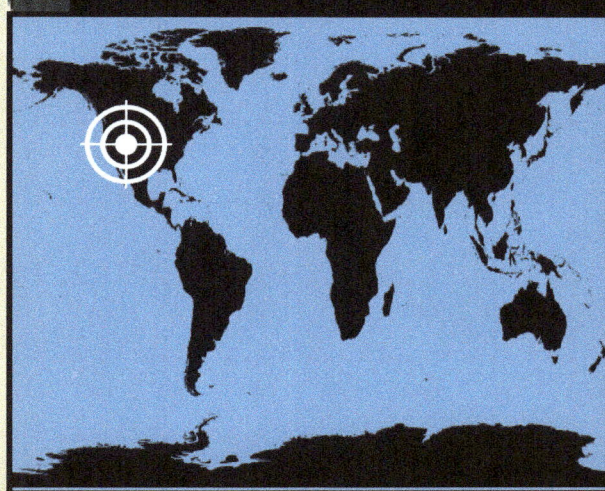

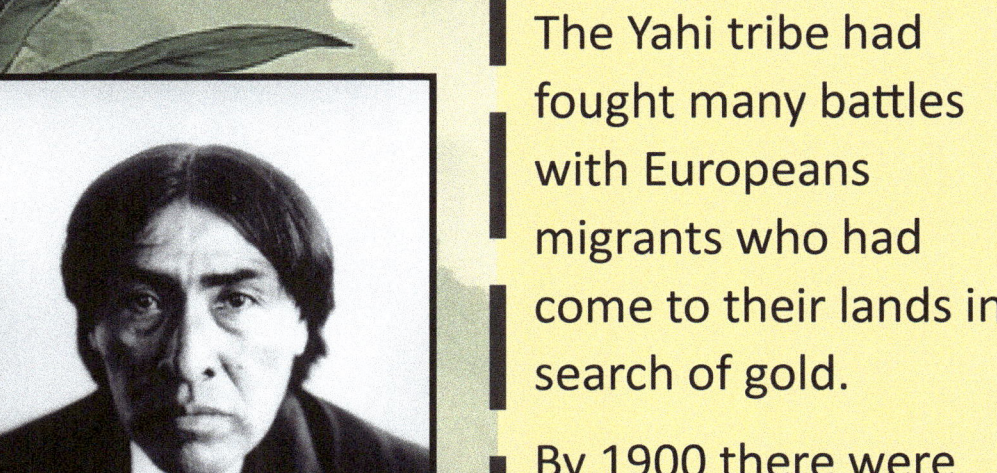

The Yahi tribe had fought many battles with Europeans migrants who had come to their lands in search of gold.

By 1900 there were hardly any Yahi left.

The last few surviving Yahi had lived in the Sierra Nevada Mountains, but by 1911 there was just one member of the Yahi people left alive. Ishi was alone and starving.

Ishi walked into the town of Oroville looking for food. The locals who found him were shocked.

He was taken to a university to be looked after, but sadly he died in 1916 from a virus.

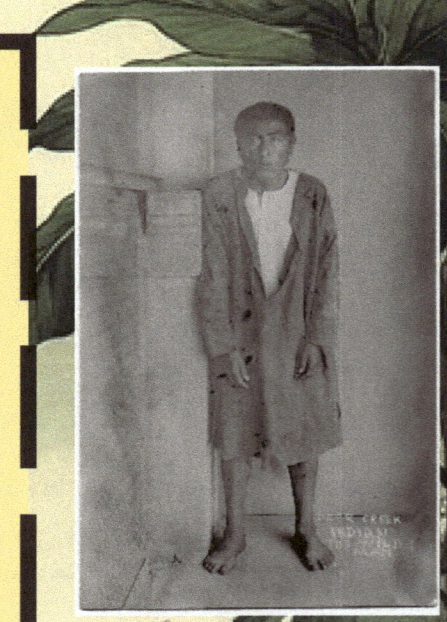

Ishi wasn't his real name. It just means "man".

In his Yahi culture he had to first be introduced by another Yahi. When asked his name he said, "I have none, because there are none left to name me." He was the man with no name.

ENVIRA RIVER

First Contact: 2014

One day in 2014, a small group of people came out of the forest and slowly approached a remote village in western Brazil.

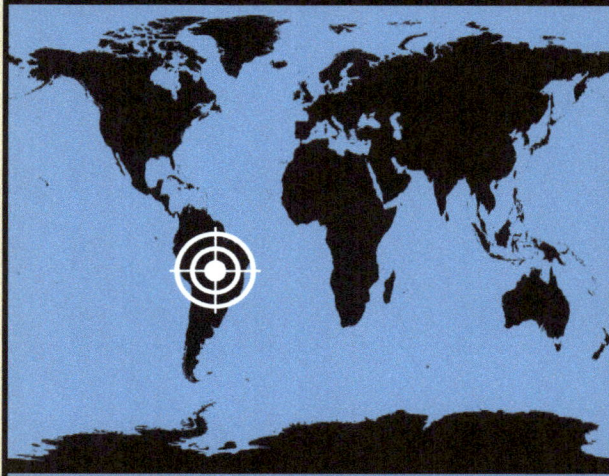

At first the villagers were afraid because the forest people were armed with bows and arrows. But they did not attack, they just tried to communicate.

At first there was tension. The forest people shouted across the river, arrows notched but not raised. This could turn out very badly.

The villagers didn't threaten them. Instead they pushed food across the river. The forest people dropped small items they had carried—maybe they wanted to trade?

But the forest people looked scared and very tired.

Did they need help?

The villagers sent a message to the nearby town and soon enough some government officials arrived. Cameras took photographs as the uncontacted tribe stepped into view.

The experts said these people were an uncontacted group of Huni Kuin people. They had been forced to flee from some loggers who had attacked their village and tried to kill the tribe.

The officials from the government agreed to help the tribe by giving them food and medicine and letting them live on protected land.

THE PINTUPI NINE

First Contact: 1984

In 1984 a family group of nine Australian Aborigines emerged from the outback and entered the modern world.

These people were uncontacted members of the Pintupi tribe who lived naked as hunter-gatherers in the Gibson Desert. They were the last aboriginal people to make first contact.

The adventure began when the group saw a small airplane and thought it was a giant bird. When it landed and people got out they were terrified and hid in a tree.

Later when hunting they met another aboriginal man. He could tell they were uncontacted and told others about them.

A search party was sent out and the family were found. They were persuaded to come to a **mission station** and were given food.

The family found it hard to adapt to the modern world. One of the boys, Piyiti, walked back into the desert. **Maybe Piyiti is still out there?**

GLOSSARY

Amazon	A huge river in the Brazilian jungles.
Anthropologist	A scientist who studies tribes and people.
Cannibals	People who eat other humans.
Loggers	People who cut down rare trees for money.
Mahogany	A rare tropical tree with beautiful wood.
Missionaries	People who want to spread their religion.
Mission Station	A base used by missionaries.
Plantation	A type of farm where only one 'cash crop' is grown (such as rubber).
Poachers	People who hunt animals that are protected or don't belong to them.
Rainforest	A type of tropical jungle where it often rains.